YOUR FIRST PUPPY

A Guide for Children

Amy Curran

YOUR FIRST PUPPY: A GUIDE FOR CHILDREN AND PARENTS
ISBN: 978-0-6484496-2-1

Published in Australia by
PINK COFFEE PUBLISHING
PO Box 483, Oberon NSW 2787
www.pinkcoffeepublishing.com

Text and Illustrations Copyright Amy Curran 2019
All Rights Reserved

National Library of Australia Cataloguing-in-Publication entry information can be found at www.nla.gov.au

All information in this book has been carefully researched and checked for accuracy. The Author and Publisher make no warranty, express or implied, that the information contained herein is appropriate for every individual, situation or purpose, and assume no responsibility for errors or omissions. The reader assumes the risk and full responsibility for all actions, and the Author or Publisher will not be held responsible for any loss or damage, whether consequential, incidental, special or otherwise that may result from the information presented in this publication.

DEDICATION

To all of the puppies who are finding their way into their forever homes. May this book pave the way to a happy, safe and adventure filled life with your little person.

CONTENTS

Introduction   6

Choosing a puppy   8

What a puppy needs   11
 - Supplies
 - Preparing your home and yard

Puppies first days at home   14

Feeding your puppy   17

Grooming   21
 - Bathing
 - Ears
 - Toe nails

Training yourself   25
 - Boundaries
 - Personal space
 - Play time

Training your puppy   29
- Toilet time
- Crate training
- Being alone
- Socialistion
- Walking on a lead
- Sit
- Stay
- Drop

Transporting your puppy   43

Health tips and the Vet   45
- Checking your puppy
- Vaccinations
- Annual check ups

Final advice and thoughts   49

About the Author   50

INTRODUCTION

So you are getting a puppy? Congratulations! Having a puppy in your life will be one of the most rewarding experiences you will have in your life time, it will also teach you a lot.

Every single dog is different, we have bred puppies from the exact same parents, the same litter, and they have had completely different personalities, needs and have needed to be trained differently to each other.

This book will not give you all the answers, puppies are not a 'one size fits all' animal, what works for one probably won't work for another in the exact same way. But, this book will make life with your puppy as smooth as can be, and give you the tools you need to ensure your puppy is happy, healthy, and a safe and friendly member of society.

Mum and Dad... this is a book for you too. It is written in a way children will understand, but please read it as well so you can see why your child is doing things, and help them where you can.

Welcome to the start of your new life with your awesome little best mate.

CHOOSING A PUPPY

There are small dogs, big dogs, fluffy dogs, dogs with no hair, and dogs with curly hair! There are active dogs and dogs that love to lay about most of the day.

How do you know which type of puppy is right for you?

Here are some of the main things to think about...

Size - small, medium or large?

Coat - long or short coated? Long coated dogs can be so cuddly, but they also require regular grooming to prevent matting. Short coated breeds can also shed hair, but don't need as much maintenance. If anyone in your family has allergies this should be a consideration as well. Some coats are better than others for people with allergies.

Where you live - Some breeds are more vulnerable to temperature than others, and some suit warm or cold environments.

Temperament - Do you want a guard dog, or a dog that loves everyone?

Will the dog suit the ages in our family? There are some breeds that are great with children but due to their size and strength are not suited to smaller children initially. Consideration should also be given to small breeds as well, as they can be more fragile than larger dogs with very small children.

Health - Are you prepared/able to care for a dog that may have greater health needs and costs than another breed, or would you be happier with a more robust breed of dog?

Getting a puppy from a responsible breeder can assist you a lot. Responsible breeders know the parentage of their puppies, back many generations, and as such will be able to answer your questions about temperament, potential health issues and care needs. Responsible breeders also carry out health tests to ensure that each generation of puppies they bring into the world are as healthy as can be.

WHAT A PUPPY NEEDS

Supplies

Take your parents to the pet store and supermarket, and try and collect these essential items before your puppy arrives:
- A bed
- A crate
- Food and water bowls
- Brushes and combs (if long coated)
- Chew toys and other special puppy toys
- Collar and leash (to fit your puppy now)
- Pooper scooper or poo bags
- Puppy shampoo
- Puppy nail clippers

The breeder you get your puppy from should be able to tell you what food the puppy has been used to before coming to you. Sudden changes in diet can upset a puppy so be sure to ask them. They may also give you a blanket that has the puppies mum and siblings scent on it, this can help settle the puppy as well. If you do get to visit the puppy before you bring them home, take a towel from your place and leave with the pupppy. This is called 'odour exchange' and lets the puppy gets used to your smells before he leaves.

Preparing your home and yard
Puppies have no road sense and they are likely to get run over if they get onto the road. You must therefore have very secure fences around your property. All fences should be checked to ensure your puppy can not fit through any gaps, or go under or over it.

It is also important to check your yard does not have any hazards within it, eg poisonous plants or substances, objects that could fall on him, or that he could fall into!

Watch hazards inside the house as well. Areas puppy could climb to and get stuck, tables he could climb on and fall off. Never leave the puppy on the lounge unattended as he may try and jump off himself.

And don't forget to hide anything that you don't want the puppy to find and chew!

PUPPIES FIRST DAYS AT HOME

A baby puppy is very much like a human baby, they need attention and time. It may also be that this is the first time away from litter mates, and therefore is not unusual that it could take some time to settle into their new home.

Plenty of cuddles and patience is what is required. Don't panic too much if your puppy doesn't eat the first day, but they may be tempted by some little pieces of cooked BBQ chicken, no bones.

This is your opportunity to form a relationship with your puppy. Patience is very important, and introduce the puppy to your other family members one at a time where possible, to not overwhelm him. This includes introductions to other animals you may have as well.

When you first get your puppy he may be a little unsettled, especially at nights. Remember he is used to sleeping with his brothers and sisters. Where he is to sleep at night must be safe, secure, warm and draught free.

If you don't have a special crate, an excellent idea is a play pen. You can then place Newspapers or Puppy Pads on the floor, which make accidents easy to clean up.

A hard plastic bed can be purchased from a Pet Store or even a cardboard box with a side cut down for access is ideal. You can purchase pet bedding that is washable.

Remember that your new puppy is like a baby and requires a large amount of sleep. They must be allowed to sleep undisturbed and have an area to go to that is theirs.

If you have younger brothers or sisters, it is important they be taught that when the puppy goes to his area he must be left alone.

FEEDING YOUR PUPPY

The breeder of your puppy should have let you know what food the puppy was used to. You can change this, but make sure to transition it if you do. It is a good idea to keep feeding the same food to avoid any upset tummies.

As your puppy grows, you may like to add more variety to his diet. Keep any treats in moderation.

You will probably want to share all of your delicious people food with your pup. After all, who can resist those puppy-dog eyes begging for a morsel? But don't give in. Some foods are just downright bad for dogs and can cause all

sorts of health problems. Some of these include:
Chocolate and Caffeine
Grapes and Raisins
Alcohol and Raw Bread Dough
Xylitol (artificial sweetener)
Onions and Garlic
Some Dairy products
Macadamia nuts
Avocados

The bones in meat, chicken and fish can also be very hazardous to your dog. They can splinter and stick in the throat, break teeth or cut the intestines.

As a general rule of thumb it is best to avoid feeding your dog human food. To keep your dog out of harm's way, stick to a diet of food specifically formulated to meet your dog's nutritional needs.

Basic feeding portion guide

Baby Puppy (8 weeks – 3 months)
The breeder of your puppy will tell you how much the puppy is having at the time you pick him up. Three meals a day. Increase the amounts you give your puppy based on their growth.

Puppy (3 months – 6 months)
Two or three meals a day. Increase the amounts you give your puppy based on their growth.

Junior (6 months – 1 year)
Two main meals a day, this may still be slightly more than what you feed as an adult.

Adult
One meal per day, we prefer to give this meal late in the afternoon.

The average puppy diet will look like the following, but please check your individual puppies needs are, as it varies with their breed, size and activity levels.

Morning
1/2 cup puppy biscuits
Fresh raw chicken or beef mince
Lunch
Fresh raw chicken or beef mince
Evening
1/2 cup puppy biscuits
Fresh raw chicken or beef mince or specialy formulated puppy loaf (chopped finely)

Be sure to clean the bowl in between meals, so your puppy doesnht have to eat any old food that is left from the meal before.

Make sure your puppy always has fresh clean water. Even if the water bowl still has some in it, it is a good idea to empty and replace with clean water every day.

GROOMING

Bathing

Please don't bath more than once a month, more frequent bathing can cause dryness of the coat and skin. Use a specific pet shampoo, as human shampoo is not PH balanced for dogs.

The laundry tub or bath is ideal to bath your dog, you can purchase a hose that has a shower rose at the end and fits to your tap. Hand warm water, as you would use for a baby, is the right temperature. Try not to get any shampoo in the eyes. After your dog has been rinsed thoroughly, dry him off with a towel. The dog must be kept warm until he is completely dry.

Once dry, finish up wth a gentle brush to remove any tangles that washing may have caused.

Ears

The ears need to be kept clean and dry. After the bath, dry the ear as much as possible with a gently with a towel. Then get mum or dad to help you finish off a gentle clean with a cotton bud. Make sure they do not poke the cotton bud too far into the ear, as it will damage the ear. If there is ever a smell coming from an ear, you need to seek Veterinary attention.

Toe nails

Toe nails should be checked regularly to make sure they are not too long. You can purchase special dog nail clippers, ask an adult to trim them for you. If your dog has black nails these are more difficult to do, as you cannot see the quick. On white nails you can see the pink quick. If the quick is cut it will bleed.

It is important that the dog is still while nails are being trimmed, so you may need someone to hold them, while you cut. Trim the nail back in stages until the nail is just slightly longer than the quick.

You can also ask your Breeder, Vet or a Dog Groomer to trim nails for you or show you how.

 The blood supply is the 'quick'

 Top cut would bleed
Bottom cut is ideal

 The quick recedes as the nail gets shorter

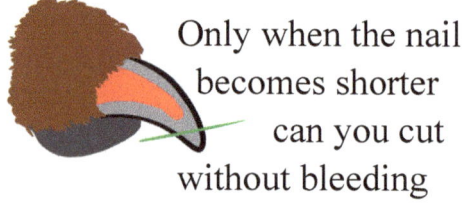 Only when the nail becomes shorter can you cut without bleeding

 A properly trimmed nail

TRAINING YOURSELF

Boundaries
Pets have boundaries, just like us. Knowing that your dog doesn't like people touching their food while they're eating or having anyone sneak up behind them is crucial information that you should remember.

You should understand your dog's personality and what kinds of behaviours bother them. You might tease your brother or sister, your dog doesn't understand teasing the same way. Animals are not humans.

Your dog should be able to eat in peace. Feed him in a quiet spot. Just as you wouldn't interrupt an adult's meal, put their hands in their food or take something off a parent's plate... you are not to interrupt the puppies eating nor play with his food.

You can give the puppy treats when it's not mealtime and away from his food bowl. During training sessions is a great time for you to give out treats as directed by the trainer.

Personal space
I hate the photos or videos that show children sleeping on top of the dog, climbing on him, riding him like a horse or otherwise using him as a toy. Many dogs will be endlessly patient, until finally a sharp elbow in the eye or knee in the rib cage sends the dog over the edge and the child is bitten.

Just as you need to learn to respect other people as you grow up, you need to learn to respect your dog. No poking eyes, pulling ears, yanking on the tail or climbing on the dog. No stomping on paws. No bouncing on the dog.

Affection in your familiy is shown to you through kisses, hugs and tickles. But did you know, that very few dogs like to be kissed on the face? Few dogs like to be hugged around the head, either.

Instead, pat your dog's back, scratch behind the ears if he likes it, scratch at the base of the tail and if he rolls over, rub his tummy. Another good place is under the chest.

Play time
Play sessions are a wonderful way for you and your puppy to interact but again, as with all other aspects of the relationship, there are some things you can do and a few you should not do.

The best games to play together are retrieving games. You can throw a ball or toy and the dog retrieves it. You can then ask the dog to drop the toy rather than taking it from the dog's mouth.

That helps protect your fingers when the dog is excited. Hide and seek games are also great, as are trick training and scenting games.

You should not wrestle with your dog, tease him with a toy or play tug of war with him as these three games tend to get the dog over excited.

Many dogs get over stimulated when several children run together. The dog will chase and sometimes catch and bite. If your dog gets this excited, don't let him play with a group of kids who are running; just put him away for that period of time.

All these warnings aside, you and your dog can be great friends. However, all friendships have some rules, whether they are socially accepted rules or rules taught for safety's sake.

Treat your dog as you would the people in your family: with respect and consideration.

TRAINING YOUR PUPPY

Toilet time

Some puppies seem to be naturals, and others can need more training. However, the best word of advice I can give you is patience.

First thing in the morning, and last thing at night, immediately after waking from a sleep, after meals or drinking…. take your puppy outside, and stay with them until they go to the toilet. Immediately praise as soon as he goes. With a lot of praise and encouragement, he will soon learn that is where you want him to go. Add a command such as 'hurry up' which the puppy can get used to and understand as toilet time.

Remember, if he does (and he will) have an accident inside, that he didn't do it on purpose. So no smacking or rubbing their nose in it. A good carpet shampoo or disinfectant will remove the smell. You can also get special sprays from the pet store to help with pet odour removal.

Be sure to clean up the accident as best you can, so the puppy doesn't recognise it as the future toilet place. Remember...

First thing in the morning, last thing at night, after waking from a sleep, after meals or drinking, take the puppy outside!

Crate training

Training your puppy to be comfortable in a crate is an important part of training. The crate is the puppys safe place, where he can eat and sleep uninterrupted. A crate is also useful for car trips, visits to the vet, or if you go on holidays with them.

When introducing your puppy to their crate it is very important to take it slow and don't rush. You want your puppy to learn a positive association with the crate. First introduce your puppy to the crate by leaving the door open so it can freely walk in and out to investigate as it pleases. Make the crate inviting by placing a comfy bed inside with their favourite toys. Encourage the puppy to voluntarily go into the crate by placing their favourite treats or chews inside while they can see you.

To help encourage your puppy to stay in the crate whilst the door is open, stay close by and try using a Kong toy filled with some puppy treats or some other eating activity such as a pigs ear or bull chew. This creates a positive association with the crate, as the puppy realises that good things happen when I am in the crate.

Once your puppy is choosing to go into the crate on their own accord without encouragement, you can begin to close the door but only for a few seconds at a time. Gradually build up the duration as long as your puppy is relaxed, remembering to continue using your Kong and chews whilst the puppy is in the crate and the door is closed.

Once your puppy is happily settled in the crate you can leave the area for a short amount of time. Gradually increase the amount of time you are absent for. If your puppy whines to begin with, stay away until he has stopped, and then you can return. If he persists for a long time, or you are concerned, you might need to ask a trainer for help.

Over time your puppy will be quite happy to go settle in the crate by its self, you can start to pair a cue each time your puppy goes into the crate such as "in your crate" or "go to bed". This builds up an association between the cue and the action of walking into the crate. Not all puppies adjust well to being confined so if you are having trouble getting your puppy to accept it, try an enclosed pen or baby gates to help puppy proof your home.

When using the crate for toilet training never leave the puppy in the crate for too long. Successful toilet training requires consistency so give your puppy plenty of opportunities to toilet outside every 2-3 hours including during the night. It will obviously help if the crate is located within earshot during the night as you will be able to hear them crying when they need to go to the toilet. As your puppy grows, you will find you don't need to take them out as often. As a general rule, puppies at rest can hold themselves for up to one hour for every month of age, however play/excitement can reduce this time.

It is beneficial to keep puppies in the crate overnight. They may cry the first night or two—in most cases, they are simply adjusting to home without their mum and littermates. Most puppies should be able to sleep through the night without a potty break by 4 months of age, but if you're in doubt, take him outside.

Never use the crate as punishment. Your dog should see his "room" as a place where only happy, peaceful things happen.

Socialisation

Experiences during the first year of a dog's life can make all the difference to their future temperament and character. Taking the time to socialise your puppy can result in a friendly, well-adjusted adult dog who enjoys the company of people.

A puppy who lacks experience with the world will find many things that we take for granted scary and is very likely to grow up to be a worried dog. A frightened and anxious dog is more likely to develop behaviour problems than a dog who has had a rich, varied and positive puppyhood.

Puppies usually go to new homes at the age of about eight weeks. This is a perfect time to introduce your new puppy to the world as they will be particularly receptive to new experiences. It is so important to continue this as your puppy gets older as if socialisation stops, they may become worried or fearful. Continue to make a real effort.

Socialisation should never stop!

How? It's easy! Take your puppy out and about as much as possible as soon as they have settled in, (and had their vaccinations) taking care not to overwhelm them.

Begin slowly at first, gradually increasing the number of positive encounters as your puppy becomes older and gains confidence.

The following are useful tasks that your puppy should learn to do. It is advised that these are done through a Puppy School or Trainer, so you can see how they are taught in person, and have help to cement the tasks.

Walking on a lead

Teaching your puppy to walk on a lead is essential. Although most dogs come to love going for a walk, they can find being attached to a collar and lead daunting at first.

1. Fit the puppy with a flat collar. Make sure the puppy is comfortable before you start the exercise.

2. Fit the puppy with a light lead that is appropriate to their size. The buckle or clip that attaches the lead to the collar should not be too heavy for the puppy's neck.

3. Hold a treat in front of the puppy's nose with one hand and move forward with the lead in the other hand.

4. Encourage the puppy to follow the treat while keeping the lead loose. If the puppy surges forward, stop and wait until the puppy turns around or stops pulling, then slowly move forward again.

5. Reward the puppy with tiny treats as you progress forward.

Get your puppy used to wearing the collar by putting it on for short periods of time to begin with. If you notice him scratching at the collar try and redirect his attention with a game or short training session to take his mind off it. If your puppy sits down, get down to his level and entice him to move forwards with a treat or favourite toy. As he moves forwards give him lots of praise.

If your puppy pulls on the lead, stop and call him back to you and praise him. Start walking again, this time with a handful of treats in the hand closest to the puppy. Lure your dog along with the treats in the desired direction, giving him plenty of praise and a treat every few moments to reward the behaviour.

Once again, if your puppy begins to pull, stop and call him back and repeat the process. Over time you can increase the interval between the treats from a few seconds to a few minutes and then longer as he starts to get the idea. This method will take time and patience but is an effective and gentle way to train your puppy to walk at your side.

Sit

1. Stand in front of your puppy and say, "sit." Be sure to speak to them in a firm, calm voice.

2. Hold the treat just above their head height, but in front of her nose, and lift the lure upward over the top of her head. To follow the movement of the toy or treat, they have to lift her head, and that puts them off balance. As their nose follows the treat, their furry bottom must touch the ground to keep from falling over.

3. As soon as they sit down, give your puppy the treat and praise.

4. Move to another area and practise again.

hint: if the puppy backs up, practice in a safe corner.

Stay

1. Ask your puppy to sit and reward her when she does.
2. Lean toward your puppy slightly, make eye contact, extend your hand with the palm facing her, and say "stay" but do not move away. Reward her immediately.
3. Repeat this several times.
4. When your puppy is sitting and staying reliably take a very small step backwards and immediately return to the puppy. Reward the puppy.
5. When the puppy can manage to stay for this immediate reward step back, wait half a second, say "good dog" and return to the puppy and reward her.
6. When you finish the exercise always give a release cue, such as "free" so that your

puppy knows it's okay to move.

7. Practise this frequently and increase the time the puppy has to stay every 2-3 days.

8. Once the puppy will stay for 15 seconds, you can start moving further away each time rather than just increasing the length of time the puppy has to stay.

9. Remember to reward the puppy with praise each time!

Drop

The puppy is taught to drop from a sitting position. Some puppies feel vulnerable when they are lying down and may be reluctant to do it. Be patient and keep the training slow and consistent with lots of praise.

1. Ask the puppy to sit and reward.

2. Hold another treat in front of the puppy's nose and slowly lower the treat to the floor between the puppy's front paws.

3. Repeat this exercise until the puppy is lying down reliably then add the verbal cue "drop". Say "drop" as the puppy's front end touches the floor and give her the treat.

4. You can gradually phase out treats but continue to offer praise like "good dog" when the puppy lies down.

5. Eventually, you should be able to use a downward sweep of your hand and the puppy will slide to the floor. Continue to reward with food occasionally to help reinforce the behaviour.

TRANSPORTING YOUR PUPPY

When travelling your dog in the car, it is advised that dogs of all sizes are in crates or carriers, both for the dog's safety and to prevent distractions while driving. If possible, crates should be secured in the back seat of a car or the cargo area of an SUV, station wagon, or minivan, and strapped in so that the crate won't slide around during sudden stops.

The crate itself should be large enough for your dog to stand up, turn around, sit and lie down comfortably, while not so large that the dog can get tossed around inside the crate while the car moves. It should also provide plenty of ventilation. You can make the crate more comfortable for your dog by lining the floor with blankets, and even go a step further to safeguard against injury by padding the sides with foam. Just be sure your dog won't try to eat or chew any material you use for padding.

If a crate is not an option, look for a safety harness that buckles directly into the seat belt buckle, and strap your dog into the back seat.

On an extended road trip, it can be tempting to drive as far as you can, but don't forget about your puppy passenger. Ask your parents to stop every two hours or so to give your pup a break, let him stretch his legs and do his business. It's also a good idea to bring fresh water and give him a drink whenever you stop.

Some puppies may get car sick so be prepared with some wipes and bags just in case. If your puppy is consistently car sick, speak to your veterinarian.

HEALTH TIPS AND THE VET

Checking your puppy
You should regularly check your puppy for any health problems. A simple look over your puppy can find any problems before they get worse, and also lets you bond with your puppy.

Eyes: observe any irregular discharge, abnormal pupil size or unusual colour of the white of the eye

Mouth: look at the puppy's teeth, gums and tongue

Ears: look in and smell the ears for any indication of infection

Outer body: massage the puppy's skin all over the body and down the legs, feeling for any lumps, bumps or scratches

Paws: check all claws for any cuts or breakages on the claws or the pads of the feet.

Vaccinations

Your puppy *should* have had its first vaccination prior to you picking it up. If not, please tell your own vet immediately, who will arrange to do this. A puppy's first vaccination is given between 6 and 8 weeks of age.

You should confine your puppy to your home for its first week with you, this is a quarantine period.

After vaccinations you must also keep your puppy confined to your home so that it has no contact with other dogs, and does not walk where other dogs may have been. This is very important as parvovirus can be picked up from an environment many months after an infected dog has been there.

The second vaccination is given at 10 (to 12) weeks of age, but the closer to 10 weeks of age, the better. It takes two full weeks to be protected from the diseases that are vaccinated against, so by giving the vaccine at 10 weeks of age, your pup can be out meeting other dogs, people and getting to know your neighbourhood by 12 weeks of age. This socialization is one of the most important times in your pup's development and the more interactions and experiences it can have while under your protective care, the better it will know how to respond to the same experience when it is older.

The third and last puppy vaccination is given at 16 weeks of age.

The first adult vaccination is given 12 months after the second puppy vaccination, usually between 13 and 15 months of age.

Annual Health Checks
An annual check up with your Vet is so important, pets age more quickly than ourselves, so for them time really flies and things can change quickly. An annual physical exam allows your Vet to pick-up on any medical problems early. You can also take this opportunity to ask questions about your pet, and discuss any concerns you may have.

FINAL ADVICE AND THOUGHTS

Your puppy will become your best friend... I dare say by the time you have read this far, they already are.

Sadly so many puppies end up abandoned at shelters or on classified sites. In the majority of cases, all it would have taken to turn the situation around was patience and training.

Don't give up on your puppy, or yourself, and you will be rewarded with love, companionship and many adventures for years to come.

ABOUT THE AUTHOR

Amy Curran lives in the Blue Mountains area of NSW in Australia, with her husband, four children and many dogs, cats, rabbits, horses and cows. Amy loves the country life, and it provides the perfect environment for raising the families award winning Australian Cattle Dogs.

The Curran family compete with their dogs at major shows in Australia, and have won many awards at Royal and Speciality level. Under their 'Table Rock' prefix, the Currans have also exported puppies to homes in Japan and the

United States of America.

Amy has appeared in Media work with her dogs, including photo shoots, and television commercials.

Amy Curran has a Diploma in Animal Psychology, and is an Accredited Puppy School Trainer.

www.ingramcontent.com/pod-product-compliance
Lightning Source LLC
Chambersburg PA
CBHW040555010526
44110CB00054B/2721